T0210111

HEROES
OF
AFRICA

Vivian Ezeife Van Gorder

AuthorHouse™
1663 Liberty Drive
Bloomington, IN 47403
www.authorhouse.com
Phone: 1 (800) 839-8640

© 2018 Vivian Van Gorder. All rights reserved.

No part of this book may be reproduced, stored in a retrieval system, or
transmitted by any means without the written permission of the author.

Published by AuthorHouse 09/27/2018

ISBN: 978-1-5462-6065-3 (sc)
ISBN: 978-1-5462-6066-0 (hc)
ISBN: 978-1-5462-6064-6 (e)

Library of Congress Control Number: 2018911279

Print information available on the last page.

Any people depicted in stock imagery provided by Getty Images are models,
and such images are being used for illustrative purposes only.
Certain stock imagery © Getty Images.

This book is printed on acid-free paper.

Because of the dynamic nature of the Internet, any web addresses or links contained in
this book may have changed since publication and may no longer be valid. The views
expressed in this work are solely those of the author and do not necessarily reflect the
views of the publisher, and the publisher hereby disclaims any responsibility for them.

authorHOUSE®

TABLE OF CONTENTS

INTRODUCTION

Africa — the Motherland — is a rich, and diverse continent with over one billion people living in 56 different countries filled with vast resources and resplendent with every color of animals, plants, and people.

Queens and kings have long ruled over the Africa where over 2000 languages are spoken. While many Africans, with many different skin colors, speak English, Arabic, or French, the largest language group in Africa is Swahili.

Africa is a land of rich stories, traditions, legends, and noble accounts – a place where a person can develop in any, and every, way imaginable. African women and men across history have influenced Africa and the entire world.

Africa is a land of beautiful, intelligent, and wise heroes of the mind, body, soul, and spirit. There are thousands of inspiring Africans whose stories we should learn, but for this study, we are going to focus on 31 great Africans,

Because there are 31 days in many months, you might like to learn about one African story each day for an entire month. Sound like a good idea to you?

Let's learn more about the amazing, inspiring, and noble heroes of Africa.

NELSON MANDELA OF SOUTH AFRICA

Who would you describe as a "living legend?" Who do you most admire? What are the qualities that make a person be "great"?

On July 18th, 1918, one of the most famous people in the world, and a Nobel Peace Prize winner, Nelson Mandela was born in South Africa. He lived through deep injustice and racism in his country. Nelson became an activist to fight injustice which led to his enemies throwing him into prison for 27 years.

In 1990, Nelson Mandela was finally released from prison. He never tried to retaliate against his enemies who put him in prison. Instead, he showed love to his oppressors. WOW! What a heroic example for all of us to follow when we respond to those who hate us.

Have you ever had a time when someone didn't invite you to their party and you were angry and decided not to invite them to your party? If Nelson had been in this situation, he would love his enemies and invite them to his party even if he wasn't invited to their party.

Nelson Mandela became the first black president in South Africa and throughout his lifetime he promoted loving one another even though the other person might look different from you. The world recognized his greatness when he was awarded the Nobel Peace Prize in 1993. Of course, he was helped by many other great and dedicated people such as Steve Biko who was tortured to death for his convictions. Nelson Mandela died on December 5, 2013 but in some ways he will never die as long as there is a free and independent nation of South Africa where your ethnic and cultural backgrounds do not keep you from enjoying freedom and democracy.

Have you ever stood up for your convictions even though it was difficult?

Place photo here

Seretse Khama of Botswana

SERETSE KHAMA OF BOTSWANA

One country in the southern part of Africa is Botswana. It's a country famous for beautiful wildlife game parks filled with elephants, giraffes, hippos, lions, and many other kinds of animals.

Botswana used be part of the British Empire. When the country gained its independence the people of Botswana wanted to see their first President be a man named Sir Seretse Khama.

Seretse was born on July 1, 1921. Most names have a meaning. Do you know the meaning of your name? The name "Seretse" means the "clay that binds together." It's a good name for a person who grew up to be a politician holding the whole country together.

Seretse was born into one of the richest families in the country. This made Seretse think about helping other people who were poor or had less money.

Seretse father died when he was a young boy. Because he was sad, he focused on education. When it was time to go to College Seretse went to South Africa and after he finished his Bachelor's Degree he went to study in England. While in England he fell in love with a woman he married. Some people criticized Seretse for not marrying someone from his own country or ethnic background.

Seretse went back to his country and brought independence from the British. He became Botswana's first president in 1966. He restored economic growth to Botswana which helped improve living conditions. After a long life Seretse died on July 13, 1980 leaving a great legacy and example for us to follow.

Seretse Khama is a great hero because of his persistence to never give up; despite the obstacles and challenges that he faced. Have you ever given up on a dream? How can you guard your dream?

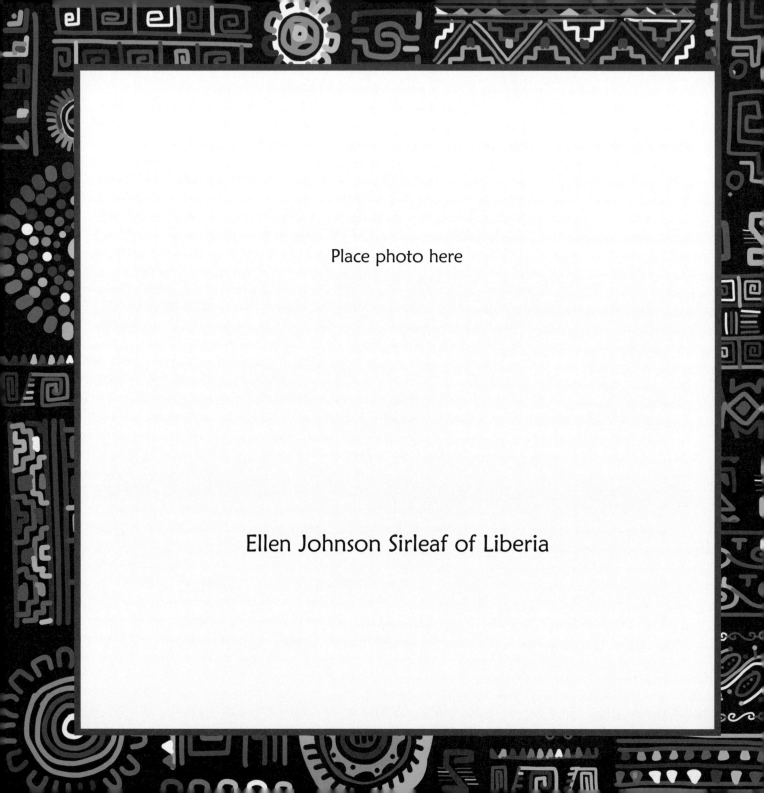

Place photo here

Ellen Johnson Sirleaf of Liberia

ELLEN JOHNSON SIRLEAF OF LIBERIA

Can you find the country of Liberia on the map? It's in West Africa. The name of the country comes from the English word for "Liberty." It has this name because some of the first people to form a government had been slaves before they were free to be citizens. The country of Liberia was founded on January 7, 1822.

The first African country to democratically elect a woman to become their President was Liberia. On January 16, 2006, Ellen Johnson Sirleaf became President. Before her the country had 24 other Presidents; all of them men.

Ellen was born on October 29, 1938 in Ghana. When she was young she moved to Liberia so she became eligible to become the country's President. Ellen grew to be a strong, intelligent, determined woman who devoted her life to public service for the benefit of her beloved homeland. She is a living example of a leader who was not limited by gender, racial background or economic origins. She overcame these — and many other barriers — to make her dreams become reality.

Ellen first studied in the United States at the University of Wisconsin in Madison where she studied business. Next, she studied at Harvard University, one of the most famous universities in the world. Ellen was convinced that education was very important and it laid a solid foundation for success throughout life. After her education, she returned to Liberia because she was determined to improve her country.

What changes do you want to make in your generation? Why is education important? What do you want to study? What college do you want to attend? How will you reach your goals?

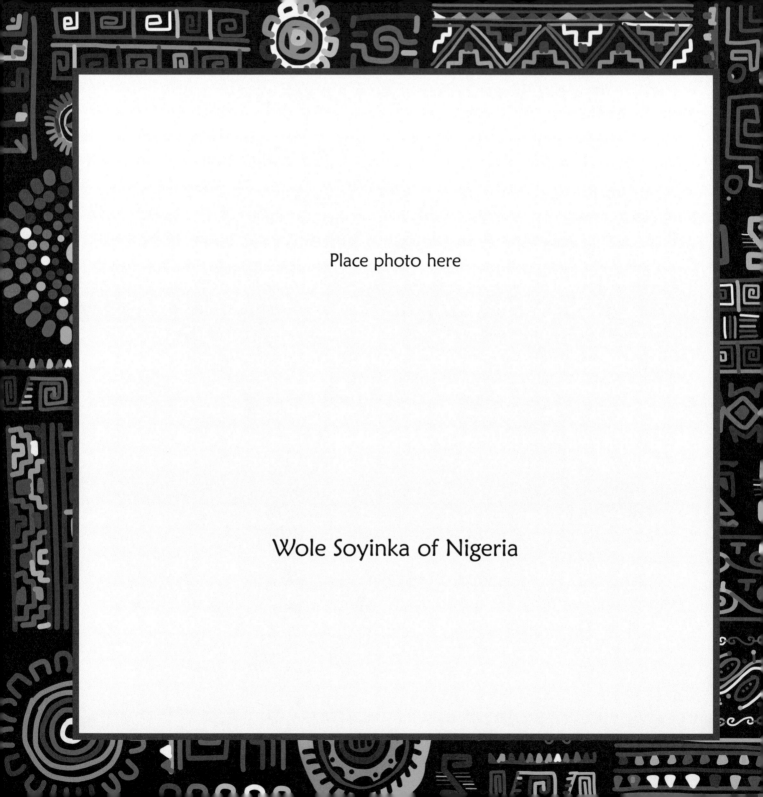

Place photo here

Wole Soyinka of Nigeria

WOLE SOYINKA OF NIGERIA

The country of Nigeria is the largest country in Africa in terms of population. It's in West Africa and used to be part of the British Empire. Because of this, English is one of the many languages spoken in Nigeria along with Igbo, Yoruba, Hausa, Fulani, Arabic and a form of English spoken in the marketplace called "Pidgin English."

Nigeria has produced many great writers such as Chinua Achebe and Wole Soyinka, who wrote in English. Wole wrote about the daily struggles of African people. In addition to writing he also worked at a university which is why he is called "Professor Soyinka."

Whenever Wole wasn't teaching his students, he wrote stories, poems, and books about the struggles of his people. His books became so popular that the most famous award in the world for writers - the Nobel Prize for Literature - was awarded to Professor Soyinka in 1987. This was a great honor for him but also an honor for Africa because Wole was the first African to win this prize.

Wole was born on July 13, 1934. When he was a little child he loved to spend his free time reading books. Sometimes, when everyone else was playing, young Wole would go read books.

As a writer, Wole wrote over 108 books of fiction, poetry and plays! Today Wole Soyinka's books are read all over the world.

What about you? Do you like to read books? What kind of books do you like to read? Do you think you could ever write a book someday? If so, what would you write about?

Place photo here

Patrice Lumumba of the Congo

PATRICE LUMUMBA OF THE CONGO

One of the biggest countries in Africa in terms of size is the Congo. It's in the center of Africa and takes its name from the Congo River; one of the most important rivers in Africa.

The Congo has many valuable minerals and natural resources and it's used to be under Belgian control but patriots united to win their nation's independence.

One of the most important freedom fighters for Congolese independence was a young dreamer and idealist named Patrice Lumumba. He was born in a farming family on July 2, 1925. Everyone who knew Patrice said he was funny, handsome, and smart. He loved to dance and have fun. Yet, when Patrice was a young man he decided to spend his life fighting for a new government for the people and by the people. Another idea that Patrice believed in was "Pan-Africanism." This idea taught Africans would be stronger if they were united.

Patrice spoke different languages and loved to write poetry. Most of his poetry is about his passion and what he believes. He also wrote poetry about his wife Pauline who he loved very much and their 5 strong and beautiful children that they both loved so much.

After the Congo gained independence from Belgium in 1960, Patrice became the nation's first Prime Minister. But, many corrupt people hated his honesty and arranged his assassination only one year later (January 17, 1961). Even today, Patrice is recognized all over Africa as a hero. There are many parks, streets, and monuments that bear his name: Patrice Lumumba will always be loved and will never be forgotten for his courage and character of honor.

Place photo here

Philibert Nang of Gabon

PHILIBERT NANG OF GABON

Maybe you like to study math or maybe you don't but math is very useful to society no matter who you are.

Have you noticed that mathematics is taught to all students from the time they are in kindergarten until the time that a student graduates from school? Even when you go to college and even if you want to study art, music, or any other major you'll still have to study mathematics. That's because learning about the basics of math is helpful for everyone and will help them deal with many of the challenges of life including helping a person learn how to solve problems and how to think critically.

There are many great mathematicians in Africa. One of the most famous lives in a small country called Gabon in West Africa. The name of this famous African mathematician is Philibert Nang, born in 1967. As a young student, Philibert loved to study math and when he graduated from college he decided to dedicate his life to studying mathematics.

This commitment paid off and in 2011, Philibert won the esteemed International Ramanujan prize on the outstanding contribution to the algebraic theory. His topic was something called D-Modules and his findings were shared all over the world. Even at the height of his fame, however, Philibert always had his heart in Africa and made it his goal in life to encourage other young African students to fall in love with mathematics. Today, Philibert serves as the President of the Gabon Mathematician Society. Philibert Nang's love for mathematics continues to inspire others. Remember his example the next time you have a math test!

Place photo here

Funmilayo Ransome- Kuti of Nigeria

FUNMILAYO RANJOME- KUTI OF NIGERIA

People all over the world face different obstacles. Some people treat women as second class citizens and as less-deserving of respect than men. This idea is called "sexism." People who fight against this idea and who fight for women's rights are sometimes called "feminists."

Many women have fought these injustices. One of them was Funmilayo Ransome-Kuti of Nigeria.

Funmilayo was born on October 25, 1900. Funmilayo grew up in a wealthy family among the Yoruba culture of central Nigeria. But, she soon realized that many laws and traditions tried to hold women back and keep them in their "place" as second-class servants to me. When Funmilayo discovered it was even illegal for women in Nigeria to drive a car the first thing she did was get in a car and prove that any woman could drive just as well as any man. She challenged the law and it was changed!

Funmilayo was not afraid of people; she gained the nickname of "Lioness" because of her fight for women's rights. She became a teacher and taught literacy. When she discovered women had to pay a tax even when they grew a small crop in their gardens she fought against and changed the law. She helped women win the right to vote. She always spoke up for people who had no one else to speak for them. Sadly, she was tragically assassinated on April 13, 1978.

Funmilayo Ransome-Kuti was a dedicated mother who raised children who were famous musicians, doctors and activists. She taught them to stand up for their rights and for those of others. Her example continues to inspire the women of Africa to fight for justice and equality. May all of us continue to work to ensure women's rights!

Place photo here

Mansa Musa, Prince of Mali

MANSA MUSA, PRINCE OF MALI

Are you adventurous? Do you like to explore new places? If you could go on an adventure where would you go?

The continents of America have had people living on them since the beginning of history but when did the first non-Native people come to the Americas? Some think it was Christopher Columbus who discovered the "New World." Others note that the Vikings left a record of their visits to Canada and the United States. But, what about the people of Africa? When did the first Africans travel to the Americas? Some believe that the first African in the New World was the famous West African king and brave explorer known as Mansa Musa, the Prince of Mali.

The title "Mansa" means king in Ghana. Mansa Musa was a brave person who loved adventures and travelling to new countries and seeing new things and exploring different cultures. His journeys took him all over Africa, Europe, and the Middle East. Mansa was also possibly the richest man in the world and along the way to Mecca, legends claim he generously distributed tons of gold to poor and needy people that he met along the way.

Mansa Musa was born around the year 1280 and died peacefully in 1337. He was a powerful king who ruled the Kingdom of Mali for almost 25 years. While he was king, he conquered many other countries. Mansa Musa is known as a person who loved learning and is credited with building the first university in Sub-Saharan Africa; the University of Sankore in Timbuktu. Mansa Musa also collected books and maps and some of his treasures still exist today! What an amazing king who lived such an adventurous life of learning!

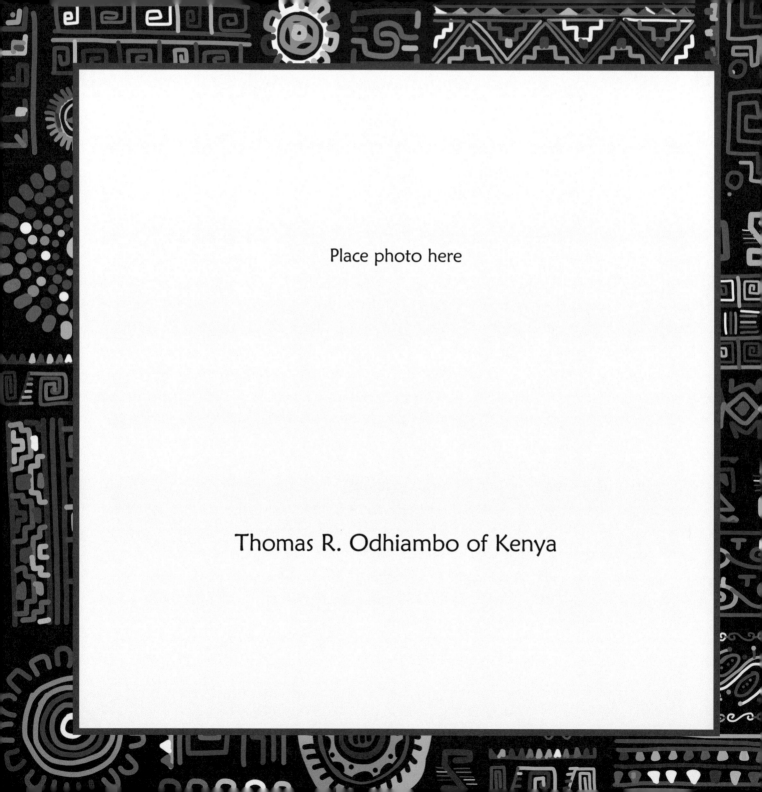

Place photo here

Thomas R. Odhiambo of Kenya

THOMAS R. ODHIAMBO OF KENYA

Thomas Odhiambo was born on February 4, 1931, in Mombasa, Kenya. Thomas was an environmental activist, an entomologist; a person who studies a branch of zoology that deals with insects.

After Thomas finished his college in Kenya he went to Cambridge University in England; receiving his Ph.D. in 1965. Thomas returned to Kenya to teach in the University of Nairobi in the zoology department. When you get a Phd., you're addressed as "Doctor." Students and colleagues addressed him as Dr. Odhiambo.

Dr. Odhiambo founded the International Centre for Insect Physiology and Ecology (ICIPE) along with Carl Djerassi. The ICIPE became a central place worldwide to study insects and how they challenge the food-security of communities. The ICIPE helped improve the health of Africa by conducting research to develop environmentally safe strategies to increase agricultural production and to address prevalent tropical and vector-borne diseases. Vectors are living organisms that can transmit infectious diseases between humans (or from animals to humans). Many of these vectors are bloodsucking insects.

Dr. Thomas Odhiambo passed away from this world on May 26, 2003 but left behind a lasting legacy in scholarship. As of today, ICIPE as been a center for scientific training which has attracted lots of scientists all over the world. Follow his example and use your curiosity about science to learn new things and perhaps make a great discovery that will make people's lives better and more healthy!

Place photo here

Great Queens of Africa

GREAT QUEENS OF AFRICA

Africa as the birthplace of civilization has been led by many great leaders. Some of these were women who left their mark on history.

Queen Aminatu was a great Hausa warrior who lived in the 16th Century. She was only 16 when she began to rule from her capital called Zazzau in what is Hausaland in modern-day Niger and Nigeria. She not only led armies in battle but also built a great set of trading routes that crossed the Sahara and extended into the Sudan.

The Queen of Sheba, Makeda, was famous for being aligned with the wise King Solomon mentioned in the Bible. She was queen over the great Ethiopian kingdom of Axum. Ethiopians believe that Makeda had a son by King Solomon named Menelik; the first of a long line of kings. Legend also says that Makeda brought back the Biblical Ark of the Covenant to Axum.

Egypt is famous for two great queens, Nefertiti who lived in the13th century BCE, and Cleopatra who lived in the 1st Century BCE. Nefertiti built some of the great tombs and temples of Egypt and was a woman of faith in the god of the Sun. Cleopatra met Julius Caesar in Rome. She also formed an alliance with Marc Antony and had 3 children with him. She died tragically bit by a cobra.

Queen Anna Nzinga of modern-day Angola was born in 1583 and died on December 17, 1663. Queen Nzinga was famous for brilliant military victories over the Portuguese who tried to enslave her people. She was also a Queen of great political and diplomatic skills.

A kind of modern "queen" was the beautiful modern model named Agbani Darego of Nigeria who became the first African to win the Miss World Beauty Pageant in 2001. She used her fame to help many people. For Agbani, beauty was on the inside as well as outside!

Place photo here

Kofi Annan of Ghana

KOFI ANNAN OF GHANA

Who is a leader that you admire? Who has inspired and led you in the past? What do you think it takes to be a great leader?

One of the greatest leaders recently in history was an African named Kofi Annan. Kofi became one of the greatest diplomats of all time but his humble beginnings were in a small village near Kumasi in Ghana, West Africa on April 8, 1938.

Kofi was a hard-working student; attending school at the Kumasi College of Science and Technology. Then, Kofi won scholarships to study economics at Macalester College in Minnesota, the Graduate Institute of Geneva, and MIT. With this strong educational background Kofi went to work for the World Health Organization and soon transferred to the United Nations. In 1997, Kofi becomes the 7th Secretary-General for the United Nations. The UN was founded in 1945 and is an international organization to promote peace, security, and human rights all over the world.

Kofi Annan was so successful in his work that he was the co-recipient of the Nobel Peace Prize in 2001. Kofi retired from the United Nations in 2006 but continued working with world leaders such as Nelson Mandela and others in a group called the "Elders." Finally, on August 18, 2018 he died in Bern, Switzerland. For all of us he is an example of how we can take on a hard job and also work for peace.

Place photo here

Janani Luwum of Uganda

JANANI LUWUM OF UGANDA

Do you know someone who always seems to be positive and keep a smile on their face even when times are hard? Are you that kind of person? Why do you think some people are upbeat and joyful while other people seem to be glum, sad, and depressed?

Janani Luwum of Uganda was always known to walk with a smile and say a kind and bright word to everyone he met. He did not live in easy times but he still managed to be joyful and positive.

Janani was born in a small village in the Kitgum District of Uganda in 1922. When he was little, he helped his parents take care of their cattle, goats and sheep every day before (and after) he went to school. Janani was 10 before his parents could afford his school fees but even though Janani was poor he still studied very hard.

When Janani was young he converted to Christianity. He spent his life working in the Anglican church to help people. He began as a priest in Mbale and then was consecrated Bishop before gaining the highest title of the Archbishop of Uganda, Rwanda, and Burundi. Janani married his sweetheart and they had 9 strong children.

At the time the Archbishop was leading the church, there were great problems in his country. In spite of dangers, Archbishop Luwum spoke out boldly against the dictator; a man named Idi Amin. For all of these bold statements, the dictator arrested Jamani for treason and threw him in jail. On February 17, 1977, the dictator said the Archbishop had been shot while trying to escape while in a car. Today a statue was erected in honor of Archbishop Janani Luwum at Westminster Abbey in London. Jamani's joyful life and courageous death will never be forgotten.

Place photo here

Rachid Yazami of Morocco

RACHID YAZAMI OF MOROCCO

All of us use batteries for all different kinds of things. Can you name some? Do you know the different kinds of batteries and how batteries work and why they work?

One of the most important kinds of batteries used today are called lithium ion-batteries. A man from Africa, Rachid Yazami, born in Morocco on April 15, 1953 was the man who invented graphite anode (negative pole) of lithium-ion batteries. Graphite anodes are used in batteries that are used by billions of people worldwide in laptops, cameras, tablets, tools, cell-phones and many other devices. One vital way this technology is used is in the medical fields and in devices that help disabled people and those with health problems.

When Rachid was young his desire to learn took him to France where he earned his doctorate degree in 1985. Even before then, however, in 1980, he made his first breakthrough discovery in the field of battery sciences.

Rachid continues to research at the Nanyang Technological Institute, Singapore. He loves to tell jokes and share stories with students as he challenges them to learn. Rachid co-authored more than 250 scientific papers on batteries and has co-invented over 140 patents that are related to lithium and rechargeable batteries. Rachid also loves cooking, reading literature and poetry and watching football. If you want advice from such a man you will hear him tell you to follow your instincts and to add hard work to your determination. Most importantly, you must follow your passions. As he said: "Passion is the fuel that keeps me moving even in the absence of tangible results."

Place photo here

Qinisile Mabuza of Swaziland

QINISILE MABUZA OF SWAZILAND

Have you ever met a lawyer? Before you can be a lawyer you have to study many years, go to law school and then pass a bar examination on the laws of your country.

Every country in Africa now has women lawyers. The first woman in Swaziland to practice law was Qinisile Mabuza in 1978. The Kingdom of Swaziland is a small country located in the south part of Africa. It is the known for its beautiful game and wildlife preserves as well as its rich proud dance and music celebrations of Swazi cultures.

When Qinisile was a student she was diligent and determined to become a lawyer. Her dream came true in 1978 when she became the first woman to be allowed to serve in her country as a lawyer. In addition to her law practice, Qinisile also taught law at the University of Swaziland hoping to encourage other women to follow in her steps.

Qinisile also became the first woman to be appointed a judge in her country in 2005. As a judge she oversaw one of the most important cases in her country which gave full and equal rights to women (2010). Qinisile was also appointed by the International Court of Justice to lead a fact-finding team of legal improprieties in Zambia. She is now active with the Common Market for Eastern and Southern Africa (COMESA) in helping to promote legal partnerships in Africa.

Qinisile has devoted her life to making and enforcing just laws. What a commitment that has helped many people! I hope you will also commit your passion to whatever career you choose to pursue. Maybe you will also be a pioneer or a trailblazer in your career in the example of Qinisile Mabuza, the first woman lawyer and judge in her country.

Place photo here

Sameera Moussa of Egypt

SAMEERA MOUSSA OF EGYPT

The modern era is known as the Atomic Age. Scientists and engineers from all over the world have been working for decades to make atomic energy safe. Even though only about one in ten engineers in the world is a woman those women who become engineers often make a major contribution. One such woman Sameera Moussa of Egypt.

Sameera was born at El Ghabia, Egypt on March 3, 1917. When she was little her mother died and her father moved the family to Cairo where Sameera went to school where she earned high grades. In 1939, she earned her bachelor's degree in radiology and became interested in x-ray radiation. As she continued in her brilliant work she became the first woman to hold a university teaching position in Egypt and also the first woman to obtain a PhD. in atomic radiation.

Of course, atomic energy can also be used to make atomic weapons and it was the vision of Sameera to harness the power of the atom for safe and affordable energy. Her commitment to peacemaking led her to found an organization known as Atoms for Peace. One of the goals of this organization was to ensure that there would not be nuclear accidents or other misuses of this powerful source.

Sameera turned down many opportunities to live in other countries saying: "Egypt, my dear homeland is waiting for me." Nuclear scientists all over the world conferred many honors, prizes, and awards on her work and for the vision of the Atoms for Peace organization. Even though she had such fame she still took time to volunteer to help treat people suffering from cancer, the disease that took her mother. Tragically, August 5, 1952, Sameera died tragically, but her great work and leadership are still remembered today. Hopefully, all of us can follow her example and work hard for peace!

Place photo here

Leopold Senghor of Senegal

LEOPOLD SENGHOR OF SENEGAL

Senegal is a country in West Africa with many different languages and cultures. Some of the people also speak French even today because Senegal was once a colony in the French colonial empire.

Do you consider yourself a leader? In the fight to gain independence from the French, the people of Senegal saw many leaders emerge in their country who showed great courage to bring changes. One of Senegal's most important leaders was Leopold Senghor. He was so beloved that as soon Senegal won independence in 1960, it asked Leopold to serve as the first President of the nation.

Leopold is most known for his poetry and his philosophical book called "Negritude" which influenced many Africans and people of the African Diaspora. Leopold was born on October 2, 1906, in Senegal. When Leopold was 8-years old he was sent to a boarding school; then, very common in Africa. Later, he won a scholarship to study at the University of Paris where he studied Algebra, Greek and Latin. Leopold also attended a seminary and planned to be a priest. Instead, he decided to study literature and become a writer.

When war came to France, Leopold was enlisted in the army but was captured by the Germans and held as a prisoner. Even in prison he used his time to write poetry. Once the war was over Leopold was given the honor of being the Dean of a Linguistics Department and France. Even then, however, his passion remained writing poetry and putting his philosophical ideas down on paper for the world to read.

When Leopold Senghor died on December 20, 2001, the world honored this great poet, writer, scholar, soldier, and President of Senegal. He was a poet writer - scholar- soldier- president. He was a man of many skills and passions; filled with energy and determination.

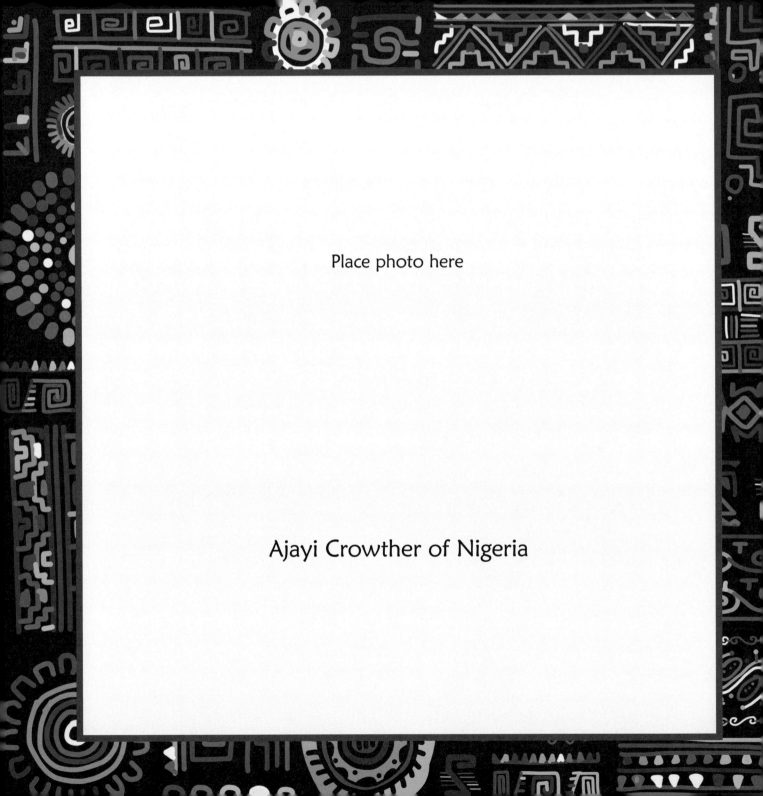

Place photo here

Ajayi Crowther of Nigeria

AJAYI CROWTHER OF NIGERIA

What was it like to be a slave? How did slavery in Africa begin and how did it stop? Have you ever read a book or seen a movie on slavery? Did you know that even today some people are slaves?

Some people begin their lives in terrible situations but rise with determination from troubles to change the world. One such person was Ajayi Crowther who was born in Osogbo, Nigeria in 1809.

When Ajayi was 13 he was caught by a Fulani slave-catcher who then sold Ajayi to a Portuguese slave-trader. Surprisingly, however, an anti-slavery British patrol boat stopped the ship that was sending Ajayi to America and he was transferred instead to Sierra Leone. There, he converted to Christianity and added the name "Samuel" to show that he was starting a new life after slavery.

Ajayi loved to learn and study and was able to learn many languages. What language would you like to learn? Ajayi loved school so much he even married a teacher! After long years in school he became an Anglican priest. But deep in his heart was a love for his Yoruba homeland so he decided to return home as a missionary.

Ajayi soon became bishop of all Nigeria spent his energy promoting education and improving people's lives by teaching agricultural and business methods. He also translated the Bible into the Yoruba language as well as creating a Yoruba dictionary.

Finally, on December 31, 1891, Ajayi Crowther died. One of the lessons of his life we should consider is how we can overcome setbacks and problems in our own lives. Even though Ajayi had been a slave he did not let the past hold him back. He is a good example for us to seize every opportunity to learn and improve our lives and change the world around us through hard-work and determination!

Place photo here

Aliko Dangote of Nigeria

ALIKO DANGOTE OF NIGERIA

Do you know anyone who has earned a lot of money? How can we use money to help people?

One of the richest people in Africa, Aliko Dangote, was born on April 10, 1957, in the northern part of Nigeria. Today, Aliko is the CEO (Chief Operating Officer) of the Dangote Group of Companies. In 2014, Dangote was listed as the 23rd richest man in the world and the richest man in Africa with a net worth of over US$14.1 billion.

Aliko was not born into wealth but, ever since he had been a small child, was driven with ambition to succeed in business. When he was little he used to sell boxes of candy to his friends at school and always make a profit.

Aliko continued his love for business by going to college to study business at al-Azhar University. Once Aliko graduated he asked a relative to lend him $3,000 to start a business in agricultural goods and services. Soon, Aliko made this small business grow into a huge company that is now a multinational, industrial conglomerate that employs thousands of Africans. The Dangote Group is Africa's largest multinational industrial conglomerate; producing food products such as rice, sugar, flour, and salt but also many other business ventures including steel, cement, and the oil and gas industries.

Even though Aliko is very wealthy he is very committed to sharing his wealth with those who are less fortunate. He is a person who gives generously to social services, communities in need, and other charities that can make a practical difference to the lives of daily people. Aliko Dangote followed his dream to business success but he used the results of that hard work to help many people in need.

Place photo here

Kwame Nkrumah of Ghana

KWAME NKRUMAH OF GHANA

Can you find the country of Ghana on the map? It is in West Africa and is famous for many things. Did you know that much of the chocolate in the world originates on bushes that are in Ghana?

The people of Ghana are proud of many of their fellow citizens but one Ghanian that every citizen of that country seems to admire is the "Father of the Nation," Kwame Nkrumah.

Kwame was born in Nkroful, Ghana on September 21, 1909. Like other great Africans, Kwame was a man of determination who fought with all of his energy for justice; becoming the first president in Ghana on July 1960. After several years of education, he put into practice what he longed for his country; that is to be independent of Britain. This happened in 1957. Other African countries followed the example of Ghana. Kwame passed away from this earth on April 27, 1972. What a powerful influence Kwame created. It shows we can set a strong example for others to follow.

One thing special about Ghana is that names are given based on the day of the week a child is born. What day of the week you were born? See below chart to see what your name would be in Ghana.

Days of week:	Boys:	Girls:
Monday	Kojo	Adjoa
Tuesday	Kobi	Abena
Wednesday	Kwaku	Akimbo
Thursday	Yaw	Awo
Friday	Kofi	Afia
Saturday	Kwame	Ama
Sunday	Akwasi	Awesi

Place photo here

Julius Mimano of Kenya

JULIUS MIMANO OF KENYA

Some people choose careers that demand great effort and education. Some people choose careers that are unusual to those of other people in their community.

Julius Mimano was the first Mechanical Engineer in Kenya and in all of Eastern Africa. Even when Julius had been a little boy he dreamed of building things. When Julius graduated from Alliance High School in Nairobi in 1955, he told people that he would become an engineer. After High School, Julius went to Nairobi Technical College, the only school in the country that taught engineering at that time, where he graduated in 1961. Eventually, he had to study in England.

In 1964, Julius took his first position working with British Railways in Kampala, Uganda. Then, he was transferred to Tanzania where he worked to build a united East African train network for all countries. Finally, in 1967, Julius was able to return home and became the senior mechanical engineer for the Kenyan rail system. In 1980, his skill resulted in him being appointed Kenya's Chief Mechanical and Transport Engineer with the Ministry of Transport.

Julius wanted the rail services of Kenya to be long-lasting and permanent and he also wanted customers to have the best freight services and passengers to have the best travel experience possible.

Julius Mimano died on November 12, 2004. There are many lessons that we can take from the life and example of Julius Mimano. He followed his dreams and was willing to make personal sacrifices to find the resources that he needed to make the most of his education and willingness to learn. He never stopped learning and always had at heart the best interests of those he was trying to serve. He became the very best in his field!

Place photo here

Wangari Maathai of Kenya

WANGARI MAATHAI OF KENYA

Can you find Kenya on the map? Did you know President Obama's father was from Kenya?

One famous Kenyan was Wangari Maathai; a political activist, environmentalist, and writer. Wangari was born on April 1, 1940. As a little girl she attended a boarding school and then Catholic High School. Wangari then won a scholarship for Benedictine College to study science before earning her master's degree in biology at the University of Pittsburgh. Finally, in 1971, Wangari became the first East African woman awarded the PhD in veterinary anatomy.

Wangari was a woman who fought for equal rights for all women. She carried on this work until her death on September 25, 2011.

Wangari is most known for working to clean the environment and starting a worldwide program called the "Green Belt Movement" which focused on environmental awareness and conservation. This movement also encouraged people to pick up litter, plant trees, and avoid buying things that are bad for the environment. Each of us can play a small part in making the world a cleaner, greener, and more healthy place for all of us to share. Have you ever planted a tree?

Wangari won many awards in her lifetime but the highest recognition in her life happened when she became the first African woman to win the Nobel Peace prize in 2004.

How did Wangari Maathai accomplish such lofty goals and reach such levels of international recognition? Wangari was a tough and strong woman. People who knew her said that - once she made her mind up she would not take "NO" for an answer. We can all learn from the determined example of Wangari Maathai.

Place photo here

King Kigeli IV Rwabugili of Rwanda

KING KIGELI IV RWABUGILI OF RWANDA

King Kigeli IV Rwabugili — The country of Rwanda is very beautiful and is famous for its volcano hiking trails. A powerful king named Kigeli IV Rwabugili was in power from 1853-1895. One thing special about this king was that he was the first king in Rwanda who came in contact with Europeans. In as much he loved trading with foreigners, he was also very smart to protect his own people from human slave traders. He made sure anything that would hurt his people should be completely avoided. He's was known as a great & strong warrior because he defeated his enemies in battle. It's amazing to have a king who cares and protects his people from invaders. When your parents ask you not to go anywhere with strangers, they are trying to protect you from harm.

Place photo here

Great African Soccer Players

GREAT AFRICAN SOCCER PLAYERS

What sports are you good at? What sports do you most love to play? Who is your favorite athlete and why?

The most popular sport in Africa is Football - also called Soccer. Many children spend hours playing football and dream of a career.

In Africa, each country forms a team that represents their country in the Olympics every 4 years and also for the World Cup; also every 4 years where 32 teams are chosen from the world's 204 countries.

If you want to start an argument ask an African who is greatest African football player of all time. Was it George Weah of Liberia or Abedi Pele of Ghana? If you ask a Moroccan they might mention "The Black Pearl," Larbi Ben Barek, once praised by Pele as the best player he had ever seen. Other Moroccans will praise Mustapha Hadji, named Africa's best player in 1998 after he helped his team score a goal in the World Cup. Algerians love Number 10, Lakhdar Belloumi, and Cameroonians love the goaltender Thomas N'kono and the dancing Roger Milla. Most Cameroonians however will reserve their highest praise for Samuel Eto'o who won many awards.

But the fans of Ivory Coast (Cote D'Ivoire) might raise the most noise. They will remind you that no other African footballer has won the award for Best African player four times except Yaya Toure and that Didier Drogba is the all time scorer and former captain of the Ivory Coast national team. Certainly, everyone in England knows about

Didier Drogba thanks to his amazing play for Chelsea where he won 4 Premier titles and scored more goals than any other foreign player. The main lesson is that we should remember is that not only were all of these people great champions but they also gave their best and focused on excellence in their sporting careers and in their lives

Place photo here

Paul Ahyi of Togo

PAUL AHYI OF TOGO

Look on a map and see if you can find the West African nation of Togo; it is a very beautiful nation noted for beautiful beaches and hill-top villages – a land which is home to almost eight million citizens.

Paul Ahyi was born on January 15, 1930, and was a beloved Togolese artist, interior designer, sculptor, and architect. Paul has built many sculptures that can be found in Togo and some parts of West Africa. He won numerous awards for his work.

The most famous work was his design for his country's national flag. What a hero! Togo has a beautiful flag. Look at it and tell what colors you see. The different colors of Togo's national flag have different meanings.The green symbol represents agriculture wealth, The yellow symbol represents mineral wealth, while the five horizontal stripes symbolize the five regions of Togo. Look at your country's flag and find its meaning.

Paul also was an architect, writer, and painter of many beautiful pictures. He did interior design and also was the sculptor of many noted outdoor artworks that are on proud display in Togo. Paul lived a productive life and when he died on January 4, 2010 the people of his country flew the flag that he designed at half-mast. This is a tradition all over the world that people have to honor those they love.

Place photo here

Christian Barnard of South Africa

CHRISTIAN BARNARD OF SOUTH AFRICA

What does it take to be a good doctor? What is the most important part of your body? Many people would say it is your heart that is irreplaceable but one African doctor, Christian Barnard, was the first person to transplant a beating heart from one person to another.

Of course, Christian could not have done what he did without help from many people. Someone very important that assisted his efforts was the great native African doctor Hamilton Naki who was also a South African surgeon who worked with Christian.

Christian was born on November 8, 1922, in Beaufort West, Cape Town Province, South Africa. After college, Christian obtained a doctorate degree in medicine at the University of Cape Town South Africa where he practiced medicine for several years.

Christian was the first medical doctor that transplanted a beating heart from one person to another. Christian also developed a safe way to detect infant intestinal atresia. (Intestinal atresia is a malformation where there is a narrowing or absence of a portion of the intestine. This defect can either occur in the small or large intestine.)

Christian died on September 2, 2001. At his death, newspapers worldwide recorded his medical brilliance. The heroes of Africa come from all different ethnic backgrounds. Not all Africans have ancestors with dark skins and that has never mattered to African people. Some African families are descendants of people from India or China or other countries. Some Africans are a mix of different cultures.

Christian's ancestors were from Europe and he had light (white) skin. This should not matter to anyone. Dr. Christian Barnard is celebrated by Africans as a son of Africa who brought honor to his country and to his continent for helping people.

Place photo here

Djimon Hounsou of Benin

DJIMON HOUNSOU OF BENIN

What is your most notable talent? How about when it comes to clothing: what kind of clothes do you like to wear and why? Do you like to go to the theatre or movies? What is your favorite movie?

Djimon Hounsou was born in Benin West Africa on April 24, 1964. When he was 12 years old he left his parents and moved with his brother Edmond to France. It was a difficult transition and Djimon dropped out of school and soon became homeless. One day, quite by chance, a famous Paris photographer noticed him and encouraged him to meet the famous fashion designer Thierry Mugler and consider a career in modeling. Djimon became very successful as a model in France and then moved to the United States in 1990. Sometimes life is like that - you meet a certain person or have a certain experience and, if you seize the opportunity, the course of your life is changed.

Djimon continued his fashion modeling career and even won a major contract with Calvin Klein in 2007. But, Djimon turned to his greatest talent which was acting. His acting career began when he appeared in some music videos of the superstars Paula Abdul, Janet Jackson, En Vogue, and Madonna. Soon, he landed some small parts acting on television shows such as ER, Alias, and Beverly Hills 90210.

Djimon began receiving major acting roles in Hollywood films such as Blood Diamond, Amistad, Gladiator, Fast and Furious, Shazam and as a superhero in the Fantastic Four, Black Panther, Guardians of the Galaxy, Aquaman, and the Marvel Comics Movies. Djimon has been nominated for two Academy Awards and a Golden Globe Award as well as winning many other major honors.

One lesson from the story of Djimon Hounsou is to never give up and to seize opportunities when they come. What are your talents?

Place photo here

Trevor Noah of South Africa

TREVOR NOAH OF SOUTH AFRICA

Who do you know who makes you laugh? How about you — how would you describe your sense of humor? Have you ever noticed that sometimes humor can be used to help people understand a serious oreven sad or dangerous situation? Who is your favorite comedian?

Trevor Noah is a well-known comedian who now lives in the United States and performs every evening on the Comedy Central Cable network called the Daily Show with Trevor Noah. This program often uses satire to lampoon the political leaders of the time and uses humor to help people better understand what is happening in politics. This program is broadcast worldwide.

Trevor was born in South Africa on February 20, 1984. He is an actor, writer, producer, presenter, and a comedian. He was raised by a single mother where moral and hard work was part of his upbringing. After graduating from high school, by 2002, he already found himself featuring in soap operas and hosting his own radio show.

Trevor has won several awards for his performances in the United States and Britain as well as in his native South Africa. In 2016, Trevor expanded his creative endeavors by writing a book of autobiographical comedy. One of the things that Trevor writes about in this book is the fact that he is of mixed parentage with his father being of European ancestry and his mother being of African ancestry. Trevor talks about how this is a positive force as he relates to two cultures.

Trevor is not only a comedian but a writer and a person who speaks several different languages. In 2018, Time Magazine recognized Trevor as one of the 100 most influential people in the world. Trevor offers a good example of a person who believes in his own abilities and has built a strong career doing what he loves.

Place photo here

Angelique Kidjo of Benin

ANGELIQUE KIDJO OF BENIN

Angelique Kidjo is a famous singer and songwriter. Her music is listened to and loved - not just in Africa - but all over the world. The kind of music that she sings is called "AfroBeat" or "AfroPop."

Angelique was born in the small West African country of Benin on July 14, 1960. Even when she was a little girl, Angelique enjoyed singing African traditional songs. When she was older she took her love of music into the school band where she soon became the star.

Even when Angelique was a teenager people started to notice how beautiful and energetic her voice was and how the music that she sang was filled with emotion. She recorded her first songs as a teenager and it was not very long before her beautiful voice could be heard all over Africa and even in Europe and other parts of the world.

There was a big problem in her home country which forced her to have to leave. She decided the best place to continue her musical career was in France. It is hard to be an immigrant but many people have to leave their country and go to a new place. This challenge can also help you to make a great contribution to your new country.

Angelique spread her love of AfroBeat music to France. First in France, but then all over the world she filled concert halls and stadiums with people who wanted to hear her sing. The sale of her albums made her very rich but the secret of her success was very simple - she loved music and followed her passion with all of her heart. She always improved her skills and soon became one of the best and most famous singers in all the world. Hopefully, you will be encouraged by Angelique's example to fully develop your gifts and skills to their fullest potential. Like Angelique, use even problems to make you stronger!

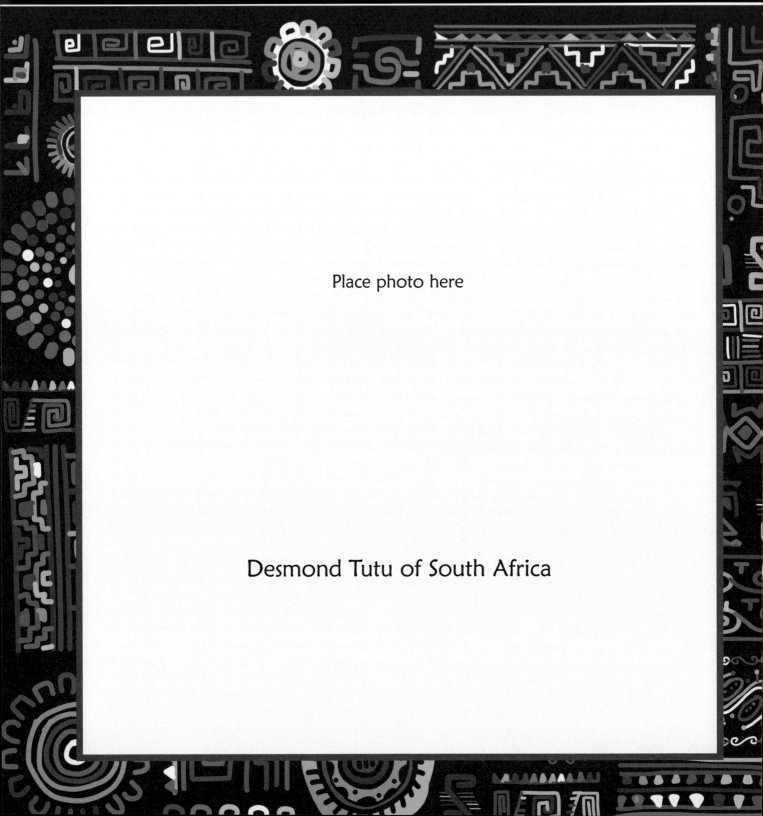

Place photo here

Desmond Tutu of South Africa

DEJMOND TUTU OF JOUTH AFRICA

Desmond Tutu was born in Klerksdorp, South Africa on October 7, 1931. South Africa at the time he was growing up followed a policy called "Apartheid" which separated people from each other because of the color of their skin. This policy of the government was rooted in racism and tried to tell some people they were inferior.

Desmond knew God had made all the people of the world in His image. He loved church and decided he wanted to be a pastor. He became a very good preacher and teacher and the Anglican Church made him an Archbishop; a high honor. For Desmond, however, the most important thing was not honors but to keep working for justice.

Finally, in 1993, the segregationist policies of Apartheid were defeated. Desmond encouraged Africans not to punish those who had oppressed them but to forgive them and work together in the future.

Even though Desmond was very famous worldwide after winning the Nobel Peace Prize in 1993, he never forgot the people of the village who helped him when he was a little boy. He was not defined by his fame or money or titles but by his heart of love for other people.

One of the lessons we should remember about the life of Desmond is that you should stay focused and stay on track and don't lose sight of your dreams for the future.

Desmond knew that if you care too much what people think about you then you become their prisoner. Even when he faced bad times he always chose to be happy. Even when people tried to hold him back he was always free. Desmond gives us a great example for us in our own lives. His example is a reminder to all of us to stay focused towards reaching our dreams and goals for our own lives.

Place photo here

Haile Gebrselassie of Ethiopia

HAILE GEBRSELASSIE OF ETHIOPIA

Have you ever watched the Olympics where the fastest and strongest and best athletes in the world come together? Do you like to run? How fast can you run? Who is the fastest person you know or the strongest athlete that you have ever seen in action?

Haile Gebrselassie was born in a modest village on April 18, 1973, in the country of Ethiopia. When he was born there was a civil war in the country as the Great King Haile Selassie, known as the "Lion of the Tribe of Judah," was in his final years of leadership.

Haile loved to run when he was young and he grew up to be one of the most famous and successful long-distance runners in all the world. Haile's ability to run with determination and persistence set him apart and enabled him to compete - at first, locally, and then, internationally. Haile won many races and competitions and never gave up in trying to be better and reach his full potential. Finally, Haile won two Olympic Gold Medals and stood on the platform to watch the flag of Ethiopia rise into the sky as the flag of champions.

Was life easy for Haile when he was growing up? Not at all. He grew up on a farm far from the city and had to walk every day six miles to school and then, after a long day, walk six miles back home. Haile learned from this challenge to be determined and to never give up! Wow! Have you ever walked six miles to school? This daily challenge gave him strength to do things with endurance.

Sometimes in your life your problems and other negative things can make you stronger and turn out to have a positive influence. What are some things that you find unpleasant but are working a better good for you in the future?

Place photo here

Ahmed Baba of Mali

AHMED BABA OF MALI

Who is the smartest person that you have ever met? Would you consider yourself to be an intelligent person?

Ahmed Baba was one of the greatest scholars of his time which was five long centuries ago. Ahmed's greatest legacy was and founding and leading the Sankore University in Timbuktu, Mali for three decades. This university became a world leader in it's time.

Ahmed was born on October 26, 1556, in a town called Arawan near Timbuktu. Ahmed's passion for learning made him move to Timbuktu as a youth to study alongside his father. There, he met a teacher, Mohammed Abu-Bakr, who had a great impact on his life.

Do you know the proverb: "Birds of a feather flock together"? It is true. Smart people will encourage your intelligence to grow and lazy people will encourage you to follow their example. This is why it is so important who is around you in your life.

Ahmed passed away to his eternal reward on April 22, in the year 1627. He was a widely-studied historian and biographer who wrote about forty books on several subjects such as the sciences, theology, astronomy, biography, and ethnography. He did all of his work at the University with the support of King Asaka the Great. We all benefit from the help of others who believe in our work.

Ahmed is considered the greatest African scholar of his era and he laid a sure foundation for future generations of African scholars. Maybe we cannot totally transform the world but each of us, like Professor Ahmed Baba can offer our own contribution to advance the world a bit further and give the world another step forward towards better days.

MAP OF AFRICA.

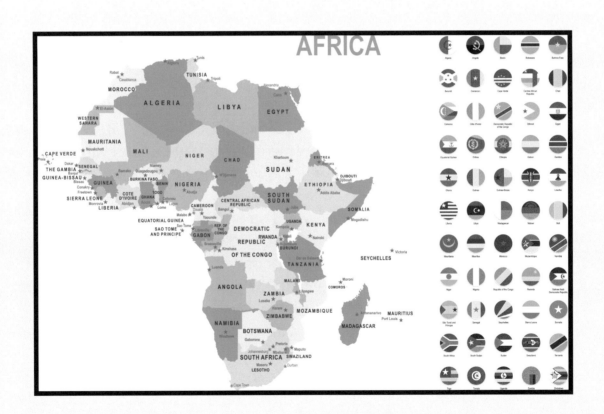

CONCLUJION - QUEJTIONJ FOR DIJCUJJION:

Reading about the African heroes that we have discussed, can you tell me what they all share in common? Describe their most notable characteristics and attributes?

Of the people that we have discussed who can you most relate to and whose story inspires you the most?

How do you think discussing the positive stories of great African people past and present can help other people from African backgrounds overcome Afro-pessimism and negative views of Africa. Pessimism.

Printed in the United States
By Bookmasters